Contrasting
English and Ugandan State Secondary Schools

Fred Sheldon Mwesigwa

FOUNTAIN PUBLISHERS
Kampala

Fountain Publishers
P. O. Box 488
Kampala - Uganda
E-mail: sales@fountainpublishers.co.ug
publishing@ fountainpublishers.co.ug
Website: www.fountainpublishers.co.ug

Distributed in Europe and Commonwealth countries
outside Africa by:
African Books Collective Ltd,
P. O. Box 721,
Oxford OX1 9EN, UK.
Tel/Fax: +44(0) 1869 349110
E-mail: orders@africanbookscollective.com
Website: www.africanbookscollective.com

Distributed in North America by:
Michigan State University Press
1405 South Harrison Road
25 Manly Miles Building
East Lansing, MI 48823-5245
E-mail: msupress@msu.edu
Website: www.msupress.msu.edu

© Fred Sheldon Mwesigwa 2010
First published 2010

Cover design: Daniel Twebaze. Cover illustration: Godfrey Banadda
Illustrations: Paul Serubiri

ISBN 978-9970-25-007-3

CONTRASTING IRONIES

"Humorously and informatively penned by a trans-Mediterranean teacher and author, this is a surprising eye-opener. The book is about a unique personal experience, based on a comparative analysis of "First World" and "Third World" educational systems. Contrary to expectations, both systems are dogged by context-specific challenges, the reality in either scenario being far from the ideal. It offers very interesting reading for all stakeholders in education, and leisure with a plus for 'all that pass by'."

Professor Timothy Wangusa

Dr. Mwesigwa went to a foreign land, participated in and observed their educational practice; and using a contrastive narrative style, discreetly avails discrete knowledge to the readers. Learning occurs from both foolishness and wisdom; wrong and right decisions; ugly and pretty situations; and from bad and good administration. Using contrasts and ironies, the book reminds us that not all that glitters is gold; and that not all that is not ours is better. It is an eye-opener for those who look beyond our borders for good things. They need a re-think. The book is an 'I-must-read' for all Ugandans, particularly parents and teachers.

Prof. Maicibi Alhas

This book exposes the starling contracts between the "First World" state secondary schools in England and the "Third World" government-supported secondary schools in Uganda. Whereas there is a total lack of discipline, indifference to scholarship and surrender of authority by teachers to students in the state secondary system in England, the state-backed schools in Uganda are known for discipline and the pursuit of excellence which are only matched by private schools in England.

Professor Laban Erapu

DEDICATION

To the students in English state secondary schools: the 'innocent'
symbols of terror and yet the victims of complex social forces

CONTENTS

PREFACE

The storyline of this book arises from my personal experience as a teacher in England and Uganda. I was particularly provoked to write following the dumbfounding irony between what I regarded as 'a First World English educational system' and a 'Third World Ugandan educational system'.

While my Ugandan teaching experience of about twenty years in government secondary schools had exposed me to a generally obedient and highly motivated student body, the reverse was true in English state secondary schools where I taught as a supply teacher in the Yorkshire region of Leeds, Dewsbury, Castleford and Morley for two years. It came as a big surprise to learn from the Yorkshire Evening Post of Tuesday 9th January, 2001 that, 'there is a chronic shortage of supply teachers. We are getting schools saying they will take anybody. There are not enough qualified teachers to replace those that are retiring'.

At first, I wondered how the teaching profession could lack teachers in a country that is a household name for scientific and technological development. Where do the many great English minds that have shaped the course of the modern technologically oriented world come from? It was chilling to consider it possible for me to strut the corridors of English schools, let alone enter the classes to teach; alas, my fears were short lived. I discovered, later on, that there was, on the contrary, a disturbing academic environment that did not easily match my great expectations. I was, to say the least, rather disappointed.

My perception of a First World educational system was of a first rate academically oriented student body. To my surprise, I was met with student apathy to education and indiscipline that was not conducive to a learning environment. Coupled with student apathy was the generally de-motivated but resilient teaching staff.

The book raises some pertinent issues concerning British educational policies and social responsibility towards children. The discussion also raises questions concerning the parameters of students' rights vis-à-vis teachers' exercise of authority and their own rights.

On the other side of the Mediterranean, the book poses questions concerning Ugandan educational reforms, which have among other things, witnessed the introduction of Universal Secondary Education with its envisaged challenges of possible increase in indiscipline and compromise of quality of education; the banning of corporal punishment in schools in the wake of new students' legislation is presented as a challenging option in a society that glorifies authority, power and respect of the teachers (call them elders). Nevertheless, the book portrays the Ugandan state secondary education system as a model in comparison to the English state secondary system. The claim the book makes about the good quality Ugandan secondary education system is attested to by Uganda's *Daily Monitor* article of Friday, July 20, 2007 that reported record earnings of $30 million from foreign students in the year 2004/2005 with $23.7 million coming from secondary school students from different East and Central African countries.

It is the intention of this book to open a debate on the best way forward in ensuring that discipline and a positive attitude to the education of Ugandan students is sustained under the new educational developments of Universal Secondary Education so as to avoid a scenario of the English state secondary schools where a free and compulsory education system, with its emphasis on students' rights and privileges over responsibilities, has resulted in students not attaching great value to education.

This book therefore highlights the irony of the British state education system that is falsely a dream destination for children in developing countries. Finally, this book is intended to bring to the fore the plight of the teachers in English state secondary schools who suffer physical and verbal abuse and are, therefore, at the mercy of students. The book exposes the predicament of students in these state secondary schools whose future on the educational journey, hence their contribution to development of English society, is likely to be dismal!

ACKNOWLEDGEMENT

I would like to thank all those who have made the publication of this book possible.

I wish to thank my dear wife and children Sheba and Shevon, Shaun and Sheba who, to different levels, had to sacrifice while I extended my evenings in office to work on this manuscript.

I am grateful to Mrs. Violet Barungi who encouraged me to look for publishers of my story. Violet was instrumental in advising me to augment the initial English storyline with a comparative element of my Ugandan teaching experience. Mrs. Peggy Noll is also appreciated for her reading of the draft manuscript and suggesting grammatical corrections. The challenge given to me by Prof. Stephen Noll, to follow up my novel with a textbook on comparative education, will be taken seriously.

Finally I wish to thank Fountain Publishers for making it possible to publish what I regard to be a humorous, exciting, informative and educative factual story that may easily be mistaken for fiction.

CHAPTER ONE

CALLED TO TEACH:
THE TEACHERS' TOOL KIT

One cold Tuesday morning, I woke up and hastily prepared myself to embark on a journey to the offices of the teacher supply agency that I had identified as a first-rate professionally oriented recruiting agency. I put on my Sunday best and armed myself with academic and professional documents. The bus ride seemed longer than normal because of the anxiety that I had to get over the whole experience.

When I alighted at the bus stage, I was greeted by a tall building that housed the offices of the supply agency. On reaching the doorsteps, there was a buzz system that I had to talk through and announce my presence. A soft but firm voice interrogated me and I calmly explained the purpose of my visit. When the door was opened, I climbed the stairs in haste and was greeted by a middle-aged lady with the characteristic English smile to say wel-come. As she sat me down to wait for a discussion with her, I noticed that about three ladies in the room were busy on a telephone switchboard answering calls from different schools that required emergency help for supply teachers. I began to realise what a big problem the shortage of teachers was.

After a brief interview with the lady with a smile, I was considered qualified to teach (perhaps in view of my teaching experience and academic qualifications plus the fact that in my country of origin, I had followed an educational system that was akin to the British educational system). However, after the interview, I was momentarily taken aback, when I was advised about the kind of resource materials that I needed to go with, to schools, while on duty. The lady in charge informed me that it was necessary for me to have several pens, pencils and rulers in case students did not have any to use in class.

For a moment, I wondered if she had mistaken me for a primary school teacher. It took some courage to ask, 'Why is it necessary to take pencils and pens for secondary school students?' She replied, 'Many of the students do not bother to bring these items, so you have to provide

1

them.' It was at this moment that I started to contemplate the possible challenges of the job. How can a secondary school student fail to have his or her own academic tool kit, with the basic instrument, a pen? Would such a student be well motivated to learn? If not, what would you expect from him in terms of classroom conduct? From the start, the attitude of students towards their education was not what I had expected it to be.

The day I started work, I realised why my boss had advised me to go along with pens and pencils. As a stream of students declared that they did not have pens to write with, I distributed more pens and pencils than expected. The most popular comment to me was always 'I need a pen.' I wondered why they were not even polite but rather seemed to consider it a right to ask for the pen to write. However, much as I tried to appeal to them to handle my pens and pencils with care, at the end of the lesson, there would be several missing. This was not because they had been stolen. In many of the cases, the pens would be lying, abandoned on the floor. Some students could not account for the missing pens and pencils at the end of the lesson. This tale was to become even more exciting when the same student would request for a pen in another lesson, if I chanced (or should I say was unlucky enough) to meet him or her in that lesson. On one occasion, there was a student who did not like any of my pens, simply because they were not 'cool enough'. She remarked: 'I cannot use an ordinary pen, do you have a better quality pen?' Since I had only ordinary pens, the day was saved by one of her mates who lent her a trendy pen. She was so serious about not writing anything unless she got a quality pen!

The tale of secondary school students not coming to school with pens and pencils was to be appreciated much later when I came across some few teachers in different schools, who set up 'mini-shops' in their classrooms. To curb the practice of students not having pens and pencils to use, the teachers sold these items to students. This, of course, is not a lucrative business, but I thought, it was an attempt at least to get the students writing during their lessons. How many times some particular students had to buy pens and pencils, I do not know, but the items were selling like hot cakes.

The story of students' workbooks was not any different. The common practice for many schools was to keep workbooks in classrooms (probably because many students would lose them if they took them home). Often the books were not up to date and some students seemed, literally, to ask for new books in every lesson. In such circumstances, I wondered how there could be progression in what they studied. The exception was easily seen when one chanced on a workbook that was more systematic and contained dated notes that spanned a relatively long period. A teacher needed to be equipped with, not only pencils and pens, but even workbooks or papers, just in case a student turned up with none. The practice of the teacher carrying basic resource materials for students' use put the educational burden of the child on the shoulders of the teacher. Without the students taking responsibility for their education, I thought, it is difficult for them to fully benefit from the educational system.

Musing over this unfortunate trend of events in English state secondary schools, I came to appreciate the Ugandan educational system, notwithstanding its shortcomings, such as lack of adequate instructional materials. While there is an outcry for teachers in English

3

state secondary schools and students' lack of responsibility for their own education, there is a surplus of teachers in the Ugandan marketplace and a responsible and generally obedient student population.

The surplus of graduate teacher trainees in Uganda has resulted in their unemployment and this in turn has led the government to phase out some teacher training institutions such as Grade Five teacher training colleges. I found it ironical that a Third World educational system can boast of a surplus of teachers while a First World educational system continues to have a chronic shortage of teachers.

There has been a long debate concerning the brain drain suffered by 'developing countries' through mass exodus of its human resource to 'developed countries'; however, with the surplus graduate teachers that Ugandan universities continue to send into the marketplace (as opposed, to say, the medical profession), it is important that collaborative effort is made between England and Uganda, for example, in addressing the shortage of teachers in English state secondary schools. The existence of historical links between England and Uganda through organisations like the Commonwealth would become more meaningful, if there was a joint effort to address such a challenge. My involvement in preparation of graduate trainee teachers and follow up after university has shown me that many Ugandan teachers find it hard to get employment and yet many of them could be made use of in a country like England.

The question of a teacher's tool kit consisting of pens, pencils, geometry sets and workbooks does not arise in Uganda. Throughout my years of secondary school teaching at Kibubura Girls SSS and Ntare School, I did not have any occasion to shoulder the responsibility of providing students with workbooks, pens or pencils. The personal responsibility exhibited by Ugandan students on their tool kits is a reflection of the value they attach to education and the learning process in general. It is, therefore, not surprising that class control in Ugandan state secondary schools is much easier than in English state secondary schools. While more time is spent distributing pens, pencils and workbooks in English state secondary schools, more time is spent in assisting students to benefit from the learning process in Ugandan state secondary schools.

CHAPTER TWO

CAN'T FORCE A HORSE TO DRINK, CAN YOU?

One of the very first schools that I was sent to in Leeds was to turn out to be one of my most challenging in the two-year period of teaching. It seems that the supply agency that I was enrolled with used the school as a testing ground of a teacher's capacity to withstand the perils of the job. Walkie talkies were being used by school administrators and teachers, not only for easy communication in the school, but for troubleshooting purposes.

Full time teachers with walkie talkies were like guardian angels to the supply teachers who they were pretty sure would receive some roasting from unruly students. On my way to the first allocated class of the day, I met several students in the corridor, who were bent on causing a stir out of every opportunity they could get. Some were attempting to trip their fellow students, others were throwing some paper flyers and other items to fellow students. There were even some scuffles in the corridors, which some teachers had to break up as they approached the classes to take the roll call. This beehive activity was characteristic of the beginning of a school day in most of the schools.

As I entered my first lesson for the day, I immediately realised that my greatest task was going to be class control and not a measure of my proficiency in adjusting to teaching in a new educational environment. There were loud noises in the class, jostling, some pushing and shoving, in short, a state of anarchy that I had not anticipated. I struggled to call for their attention and it was like pushing against a wall. One student offered me 'some advice' and said, 'shout at them, that is when they can listen to you.' It was a difficult moment for me since my prior teaching experience had never involved having to strain my vocal cords to out-compete students' noises. I thought that it was crucial to devise some cunning strategy that would enable me to catch their attention.

While some students shouted, many directed a barrage of questions at me. 'Where do you come from?' 'Which football club do you support?' 'Do you smoke?' I soon realised that their curiosity was on their personal interests of evaluating who I was, what my interests were, instead of what they expected from me as a teacher. Anyhow, I used their questions as a means to establish rapport with them and gave them some brief answers to satisfy their curiosity. The lead question that I considered more important, was one concerning where I came from, as a means of exciting them about why I had to travel overseas to fulfil my academic ambitions. Generally, the academic talk did not seem to be a cool subject except for the interest in African geography, culture and weather. Nevertheless, I was able to arouse their interest before I introduced the academic task of the day.

As I explained the day's task for an English Language lesson, there was excessive noise from the class next door. The adjoining wall between the two classes was not sound proof and it became almost unbearable for me to communicate to my students. The students in the next class kept on banging against the wall so hard that some of my students suggested that we go there and bring some order. It was a sarcastic remark since they knew that there was a full-time teacher in the class.

However, it was almost a realistic suggestion in view of the disruption caused to students in my class. At this point, some of the unruly students in my class used the opportunity to make more noise. The teacher in the class next door made use of her Walkie Talkie and called in 'reinforcement'. What was particularly interesting is that even the most callous of students would cow at the mention of a senior administrator coming. Nevertheless, the unruly students in the class next door and my own were handed over to the authorities for 'cross examining' and other procedural matters that I did not follow since I had to move to a new station.

The events that unfolded in my very first lesson and whose pattern was similar throughout the two years of my teaching reflected a majority student population that was disinterested in their education. The English Language lesson that comprised of simple exercises on sentence construction was not responded to with gusto as I had anticipated. Although the exercises were rather simple for the year eight class, many students had real difficulties in accomplishing them. However, they did not ask for assistance. I started to realise what a monumental task it was to excite students into fulfilling the academic targets expected of them.

The main occupational hazard of teaching seemed to be putting up with a majority student population that was largely apathetic to studies. No sooner had the lesson began than the students started making appeals for packing up (a reference to winding up the lesson's activities). It dawned on me how a full-time teacher, like the one next door, could be having problems of indiscipline with his students. I also understood why I had been asked to cover for a teacher who was probably seeking a break from the volatile school environment.

The psychological torture I suffered at the hands of the students at my first state secondary school workstation helped me to internalise what it meant to teach in such schools. I was able to fully understand why the teaching profession was not overflowing with teachers. It would take nerves of steel to teach and complete a school day without regretting belonging to the 'noble profession' of teachers. At no time in my Ugandan teaching experience had I ever entered a classroom and students refused to listen to me. I came to realise that in a way the Ugandan students are a captive audience who are ready to listen and learn and this seems to arise from their respect of the elders and the social-cultural and religious ethos!

The major interest of English state secondary students in wanting to know my country of origin, favourite football club or favourite musical artist contrasted sharply with that of their Ugandan counterparts who were hungry for the completion of the curriculum. While any professional teacher needs to have occasion to have a laugh with students over some trivial issues concerning a teacher's interests and hobbies, it is not the norm in Uganda as seems to be the case in England.

In my Ugandan teaching experience, I remember a few cases when students complained about teachers who were fond of telling them funny stories instead of teaching them according to the syllabus. It is not uncommon in Ugandan secondary schools for students to protest against teachers whom they consider incapable of teaching well. There is no single incident that I ever came across or heard about in the English state secondary schools where students had complained about a teacher who was not up to scratch. The reality, of course, is that it is only students who are academically alert (including some who may read ahead of the teacher) who may detect loopholes in the proficiency of a teacher. Some teachers often do not prepare adequately for their tasks and it would take good students or a good administrative system to expose such teachers, which was hardly the case in the English state secondary schools.

CHAPTER THREE
NOT COOL TO BE A GEEK

On one of my visits to a school outside the city centre, I was introduced to new vocabulary that was to epitomize the general attitude of most students towards excellence in the academic world. As I was pacing up and down a year nine class (the equivalent of Ugandan senior three) and checking on students' work, a row erupted from one of the corners of the classroom. When I moved over to sort out the problem, a group of three pointed an accusing finger at one boy. Despite the accusations regarding the boy's conduct, it seemed unlikely that he had actually offended any of them. He later told me that the other students got on his nerves for disturbing him, in class. During their verbal exchange one student called the boy a "geek".

While trying to calm the boy, who seemed to have had enough of his colleagues' behaviour, he confided in me that some students often molested him and called him names because he did not tolerate any nonsense from those who wanted to disrupt him. The boy told me that his positive attitude to studies had earned him many enemies in the class. It seems that he was considered a social misfit, as he was not willing to join in the paper plane games, notes and crosses games and other cheeky habits that other students engaged in.

I was disheartened by the fact that the boy's determination to study may not come to fruition since it might be difficult for him to put up with such torments, jeers and sneers from his classmates. A similar incident was to happen in another school, where a new student from another school, who showed zeal for studies, was being tormented by her colleagues. When I asked her, she simply said, 'Students are not happy that I show seriousness with my studies. They want me to be as playful as they are'.

As I was later to learn from a conversation with other students, the word "geek" is a reference to an intelligent student, with connotations of being ugly or not being cool. What a misfortune it is to be intelligent, I thought. But, the question is, is it really true that intelligence is synonymous with ugliness? Where on earth do students derive this theory? Perhaps, I thought, their minds were mainly coloured by the pop star world that they idolised. Excellence to them was probably more easily defined by musical or football stardom. How about Nobel Prize winners in science, medicine, literature and other fields, a proportion of which are English? Do these students ever hear about them? Do they not consider them cool for making outstanding achievements in different fields?

The highly motivated "geek boy", in contrast with the disinterest shown by many of his colleagues, reminded me of a research study that I carried out in 1998 in a state secondary school in another part of England, while pursuing my second degree. At the time, I was particularly struck by what I considered to be low aspirations of secondary school students who filled in questionnaires based on a gender related topic.

The majority of students (male and female) in the study indicated their dream jobs, were 'local artisan skills' oriented instead of 'traditionally high sounding' academic oriented jobs. Although my disappointment at the findings was explained away by one academician, who argued that it was a reflection of the inner city status of the school, I had to take in the explanation with a pinch of salt. I wondered why students from socially deprived areas were not motivated to rise above their parents' station in life. Is it lack of professional teachers? Is it lack of facilities? Could the answer lie in the student's world view that it is not cool to be a geek? Is it because the educated are not highly rated by society, or accorded 'due respect', or granted good remuneration by the political establishment? Is it lack of an academic competitive spirit in the classes? Indeed, there seems to be a deliberate effort to try and ensure that all students feel 'valued' for their capabilities by promoting students to the next class. This is irrespective of performance and avoid acknowledging excellence by not ranking students. Perhaps, this is the reason why the "geeks" are viewed with an evil eye since they are seen as being in a class above the rest?

In Ugandan state secondary schools, students who perform well academically are normally highly respected by their peers and staff and are more often than not elected by their mates for student leadership responsibilities. The rationale in giving leadership responsibilities to academically good students is that they immensely contribute to a classroom environment conducive for learning. As prefects, they can ensure class control even in the absence of a teacher.

It is common practice in Ugandan state secondary schools for staff and even students' bodies to approve hard-working, well-behaved and academically sound students as leaders. The respect given to the Ugandan geeks indicates the value attached to education and the pursuit for academic excellence by the school community. More often than not, these students give guidance and counsel to their class or schoolmates and contribute to a serene classroom environment even in the absence of teachers. While the English "geek" is an endangered species, the Ugandan "geek" is respected and supported.

While students who are academically good in England are described with derogatory terms, such as "geek" with connotations of being ugly or weird, such students in Uganda are not only respected for their academic prowess but given names that can boost their self-esteem. In a Ntare school magazine published in 2000, there is a Ntare school vocabulary page outlining thirty jargons used by students. Although most of the jargon referred to terms used in social relations between the students, some of it referred to their academic life. A student who reads his books a lot is referred to as *Okwasi*; another term is given as *Omukwasa* meaning one who reads hard. Another term given for a bright student is *Omucweezi* which is a reference to a mythological demigod who ruled over the land of Ankole where Ntare school is found.

The plight of the geeks in English state secondary schools may partly be a result of the educational policy that does not encourage the progressive assessment of students' academic work by awarding marks and giving positions in class. Since every student is automatically promoted to the next class, there seems to be no need on the part of students to work doubly hard. Why would a student spend extra hours at night to read when he or she is assured of being promoted to the next class whether or not they pass their exams? This thinking might be key in influencing students to consider alien any students who work hard and want to excel. Differences in performance between individuals is a reality of human experience and stifling it in the interest of achieving false academic equality runs the risk of stunting the academic potential of many English students.

The positive attitude that students in Uganda have towards a healthy academic competition in class is responsible for the highly motivated student body. Ugandan students in rural and urban areas have always aimed higher in their academic endeavours to the extent that some have been over ambitious. While it is very common to come across secondary school students with dreams of joining the university for courses like engineering, medicine, Law, or Mass Communication, it is rare for most students in English state secondary schools to have such dreams. While reporting on a project by Leeds Metropolitan University students to inspire local secondary school students to go for further education, an article in the *Leeds Student* newspaper quotes a Leeds career development officer commenting on the aspirations of students of one of the secondary schools in the area thus:

'On average, only one in 90 of these children will go on to higher education. Many kids we meet don't know anyone in higher education at all and we want to show them that there are opportunities there.'

The grim statistics and the low academic aspirations of students in the English state secondary schools referred to reflects the general picture in state secondary schools that I visited. It was surprising that, in almost all schools, very few students that I met seemed to have aspirations of going beyond secondary school education. I was once told by an English friend of mine that the most popular question of year ten students to their mates who may nurse ideas of taking advanced levels is, 'You mean you are staying on?' Implying that it would be surprising for a student who has completed his General Certificate of Secondary Education (equivalent to Ugandan Ordinary Level) to continue for Advanced Levels. In short, there is no motivation to continue and benefit from higher education and, therefore, the students are condemned to a life of low skilled jobs. Whatever the possible causes of apathy to education, high level academic achievement on the part of many is yet to be yearned for.

CHAPTER FOUR

SKIVING AND FALSE ALARMS

Although the failure of students to attend school may be a result of genuine excuses, it seemed that many students avoided school because, according to them, it was boring and probably, not cool. The sarcastic comments that often accompanied the mention of a student's name, who was absent, often had a lot to say about the reasons for absence. This was particularly the case with respect to certain students, who seemed to make a habit of it. The attractions of the outside world, seemed to be more compelling to these students than those inside a classroom. I wondered why students shunned a free education that had prospects of turning their lives around, let alone their fortunes.

One of the most common remarks that accompanied the mentioning of names of absent students, while reading the register, was the chorus response of skiving. It was interesting to note how, oftentimes, students in the different schools used common terminology to describe their actions. Skiving was one of them and the other chilling out!

While the students who came to school could be applauded for not playing truant, some of them would come determined to stir things up during the day. One of the most frustrating antics of students, at least in two of the schools that I visited, was the setting off of false alarms during study sessions. It was particularly annoying when false fire alarms were set off, sometimes three times in a day, which meant that students would have to get out of classes and head for the assembly points. Although teachers were expected to know the whereabouts of their students at any given time, the students who set off the alarms often eluded them.

This form of disruption to the school timetable never seemed to cease for the time I spent at these two schools. On one occasion, a science teacher of one at the schools lamented the disruptive effect of false alarms to her lesson plans, especially whenever she was in the middle of carrying out experiments. Indeed the disruptions were costly in terms of lesson plan coverage and thereby students' effective learning.

I actually considered it a blessing in disguise that some of the disruptive characters played truant more often than not. It would probably have been worse for the whole class if they came regularly. The students who were determined to study for a bright future were forced to endure such hurdles from their unruly fellow students.

It is very possible that this unruly behaviour takes its toll on the well-behaved students. Some of them might even play truant instead of coming to school to face torment and bullying or to put up with disruption of lessons. The reasons for playing truant are, therefore, likely to be multi-faceted and this might partly explain why many students keep away from school. The schools, however, try to encourage good attendance. Upon my visit to one school on a Friday, the school administration handed me some prizes for the students who attended classes for a whole week without missing. The prizes for a year eight class (the equivalent of senior two in Uganda) included rulers, pens and sweets (never mind the negative health implications).

What was perplexing to me, more than the ploy of encouraging students to attend, was that this was an indicator of a crisis that had led staff to design measures of motivating students to attend. I wondered how a secondary school student had to be bribed to attend school with sweets just like a nursery child. Whose future was at stake, the students in view of their job prospects, or the school in view of inspection reports? I thought it was a pity that secondary school students could not realise the benefits of attending school. I realised why students' vocabulary was characterised by words like 'who cares' 'doesn't matter' 'never mind' and the like. I continued to marvel at the way students believed the world owed them a living while they did not seem ready to make a difference in their own lives. I thought, if there was to be any starting point of encouraging attendance, it had to be directed to the attitude of the students towards the benefits of education.

The students do not take examinations seriously either. On one of my visits to state secondary schools, a senior manager came to my class looking for eleven-year-old students who had dodged GCSE mock exams. These students had chosen to attend other lessons with other year groups instead of sitting the mock exams. The senior manager went around fishing students from the different classes and convincing them to go and sit their exams. I was later told by some of the permanent staff that at the school, it was not uncommon to dodge even the final compulsory GCSE exams.

While it is rare for a Ugandan student to dodge mock exams or national examinations (almost unheard of throughout my teaching experience), it would be an exaggeration to argue that there are no cases of students who play truant. However, it is generally true to say that my experience of students who skive lessons in Uganda is not anywhere near my English state secondary school experience. The 2000 Ntare school magazine has one word *Okuzwisa* for skiving lessons (compared to three words for academic prowess) an indicator that skiving is not a foreign idea in Uganda, however, the magnitude is the issue for debate.

The concerted effort of parents in ensuring that their children attend school is one of the reasons for the low truancy levels in Uganda. An interesting dimension to the motivation of parents seems to be the hefty sums of money they pay for the education of their children. It is a great investment that parents make when they pay fees and, therefore, they consider it important to monitor their children's progress. Hence, there is a strong bond between the teachers and parents through organisations like the Parents Teachers Association.

In England, where secondary education is free, there are no clear accountability obligations of reporting about students' performance between students, parents and staff. The students do not feel duty-bound to give an account to parents since it is the government that meets the cost of their education. The teachers who are paid by the state do not seem to have express obligations to give accountability to parents who do not directly pay their salaries (much as the salaries are met through taxation which parents contribute to).

The students, on the other hand, do not seem to have accountability obligations to the government that supports their education since the government is rather distant and its influence can easily be felt. With the onset of Universal Secondary Education in Uganda, there are great fears among some educationalists that the quality of education will plummet and discipline is expected to be the first casualty. The element of meeting the cost of education by parents in Uganda's state secondary schools, while not being a magical solution to Uganda's educational and social needs, had maintained a state of affairs where education was a prized possession by all and sundry.

CHAPTER FIVE

THOSE WHO CAN, CAN'T TEACH

In my conversation with a newly qualified teacher whom I met at one school, I became convinced that many people who can teach, will not take up what is often referred to as a noble profession. The young Art teacher, who was in her early twenties, vowed never to teach in secondary schools after qualification. Instead, she planned to tour primary schools and conduct demonstration lessons. Students at the school had disrupted her lessons and left her in deep emotional pain.

The morning that this teacher was angered by students, I happened to be in a class next door and my own students had not been any better. The difference, in my case, was that I was by then 'senior' in the job and knew how to diffuse a bad situation in any uninviting class. From what she told me, the students kept shouting, and pushing each other and it was difficult to get them to keep quiet. Another major problem was that they had insisted on playing some music while they went about their given tasks. This was, and continues to be, an acceptable practice in most schools provided that the music is at room level. However in their case, they had not even listened to her instructions and straightaway wanted to listen to some music. Somehow, she managed to complete her lesson but the experience was not a good one.

When I went to the same class in the afternoon, I tried to establish rapport with the students by asking them why they had been disrespectful to the Art teacher. One student said, 'She is dumb, she can't speak'. When I asked the student, 'Did you listen to what she had to say?' The boy went numb! I went on to give them a lecture on positive behaviour and its benefits. Of course it fell on some deaf ears but I believe some students appreciated the talk. I noticed that many students realised they had erred in 'shouting down' a young lady teacher, especially since she belonged to the rare species that is much needed to invigorate the teaching profession and make it more *cool* in student speak.

I also had my fair share of 'running battles' with the students but I was disheartened when the young lady Art teacher would not consider becoming a full-time teacher to pursue the job she had qualified for. It is possible she had expected things to be different. Or, perhaps, she was educated in independent schools and did not know the magnitude of the problem in state schools. On the other hand, I thought, she probably went through a state school and considered this pay back time. Maybe, she had given her teachers a rough time. There was also a chance that she was one of the well behaved students who had overcome the challenges of the state education system. Whatever the case was, a young lady who in my estimation had the qualifications and capacity to teach, was not willing to because of the uncontrollable behaviour of students.

One time, I left school on a bus with a group of year nine students. I engaged them in a conversation and though could not verify their story, it was quite revealing about their mentality. They recounted an incident when they intimidated a newly qualified teacher. Apparently, they had told the teacher: 'You are welcome to our class but you must behave. If not we shall make life difficult for you. You know the teacher before you refused to cooperate with us and we accused him of touching a girl's hair and things like that, and we won. He was dismissed!' The account of the students, even if it was imaginary, said a lot about their indifference to studies and their desire to make teachers toe their line. It is for this reason that young newly qualified teachers refuse to teach since the student is the 'boss' and the teacher 'the servant'.

One of the distinctive characteristics of the teaching staff, full-time and supply, is the age of teachers. It would seem that secondary school teachers are, mostly veteran teachers who are in the range of fifty years and above. It is not common to come across young men and women. Although my physical features can pass for a twenty year old while I am forty-four (I was told so countless times in England), I was fascinated by the fact that many students thought it was odd for me to have chosen the teaching profession. It seems the teaching profession is synonymous with old age.

On one occasion, a supply teacher colleague of mine, who had grey hair and looked old, confided in me how students had made fun of him. They taunted him saying, 'Why are you teaching us, you are fit to be our grandpa!' He remarked that it was so unfortunate that the students did not even realise in the first place why young teachers were not enthusiastic to teach them. It must have been a testing time for the veteran teacher but like any old guard, he knew how to play his cards and successfully finished his lessons for the day.

The greatest motivation for the 'grandpa' teacher was paying fees for his daughter. 'I am getting ulcers from this job man', he said. 'If it was not for my daughter's university education, I would be off it now!' This incident showed me the attitude of students who did not appreciate the old man's sacrifice. They should have respected him for responding to the desperate call of a desperate agency that was responding to a desperate need for teachers, by a desperate school administration.

In a conversation that I had with some fellow overseas students, who were also professional teachers, it came to light that many of them had shunned teaching in English secondary schools, despite the attractive pay package. Some of those who had enrolled and been deployed gave up on the very first day. One professional teacher managed to teach for about four months but later gave up and, in spite of his Doctor of Philosophy degree in English Literature, I left him working in the post office in the sorting department!

The overseas trained teachers' biggest problem seemed to be the English students' negative attitude towards their education, reflected in their lack of respect for teachers. Most of the teachers had given up, without even trying because of the stories their predecessors told them. The lack of people to take up supply teaching or full-time teaching, was very evident to me when, during crisis, supply agencies would call upon me to go to some schools and yet I could not go because of my own academic pressures.

While not every overseas teacher qualifies to teach in English schools, several of the qualified ones are put off by the students' bad behaviour. The vigorous campaign messages aimed at teacher recruitment which are splashed on local buses – 'Those who can, teach', 'Take the buzz to school' – are likely to be ignored by most national and overseas teachers.

One wonders what would happen if all the teachers over fifty were to retire; would secondary schools close their doors to the students? Would the unruly students celebrate? With the majority overseas teachers not being in position to teach, the newly qualified teachers, as in the case of the lady Art teacher and the possibility of an abdication of duty by the old guard, those who can, may not teach.

The contrast between the age groups of English state and Ugandan secondary teachers is telling enough of what an endangered species the English secondary school teachers are. While in English state secondary schools it is not common to come across youthful teachers, in Uganda it is the prevalent age group. The older one becomes, the more insecure one becomes on one's job, since the students will increasingly favour youthful teachers to old teachers and the good thing is that in Uganda the former are not in short supply. Between the two government secondary schools where I taught, there were only about three teachers who were over fifty out of a combined staff of about ninety!

The presence of many young Ugandan teacher trainees has greatly helped in bridging the gap between staff and students. The students find it easy to relate to and respect teachers who are not that distant in terms of age. This creates a rapport between the teachers and the students, enabling them to communicate effectively with each other. Although the age of the teacher may not be a key determinant of how proficient a teacher is, it would be ideal if younger teacher trainees are encouraged to join the profession. The harassment meted out to newly trained Art teachers however, prevents the majority English youth from considering enrolling for the noble profession. This needs to be addressed urgently.

CHAPTER SIX

A CLASS FROM HELL

Rarely will any full time teacher warn a supply teacher about the students' behaviour. The full time teacher prefers that the supply teacher finds out the hard way. On one of those rare occasions, a Mathematics teacher, whose lesson I was to cover, warned me about the indisciplined students in her class. She said: 'Be prepared to meet a class from hell.' I was shocked and filled with disbelief at her lack of confidence in the class. She armed me with a register and noted with a red pen the 'arch-devils' who were most likely to give me a hard time.

The Maths teacher went along with me to introduce me to the year nine class and showed me around before proceeding to a meeting. During her brief stay in the class, I realised why she had called it a class from hell. She spent a lot of time trying to shout the students down as they kept playing and fooling around with all sorts of tricks. I thought if the students could behave in such a manner before their own teacher, what chances of survival did a supply teacher stand? However, when she left, I took charge of the class and went through what I considered to be the normal procedure of establishing rapport with the students before engaging with the task at hand.

Surprisingly, the lesson progressed relatively well and did not produce any over the board behaviour. Perhaps, the Mathematics teacher had pity on me and thought that I had not been acquainted with the unruly behaviour of students in English schools. Or, she was merely unfortunate in her failure to get along with the students who are picky about whom to respond to or reject. But I also thought that maybe it was my lucky day to survive the class from hell. The one thing that struck me about this incident was the teacher's resigned attitude towards her students. It was evident that she had given up on them since they were not ready to listen to her and attend to their work. It was difficult to see how the students were going to benefit from their Mathematics lessons with a teacher who had lost hope in them. Her attitude towards them was hardly conducive for effective teaching. The students' attitude to their teacher was hardly effective for learning either.

I encountered a similar incident regarding a teacher's attitude in another school. While briefing me on the lesson cover that I was to conduct for a Geography teacher who was away, a Physics teacher blurted: 'Be on your guard, the students in this school are s***.' I was later to discover that there were serious problems of teacher retention in the school due to the unruly conduct of students.

It seemed as if the abusive teacher had just had a row with some students although the school day had just begun. The swear word he used in reference to the students did not reflect any gentlemanly behaviour. For the first time, I thought, the teacher was the foul-mouthed one and guilty of displaying a negative attitude to his students. If given time, of course, he would have justified his anger and disappointment at the students.

As the school day kicked off, I was to appreciate the Physics teacher's disappointment with the students of the school, though not his foul mouth and negative attitude. On that day, two year seven boys started a fight in my class. It was so astonishing because it was the first time this happened to me. In addition, in most of the schools I taught, year seven students were normally calm, although not saintly. The ones in this school were different.

The fight broke out from what seemed to be a slight provocation of one student by another. It was a very tough situation to contain and I had to restrain the two boys from hitting each other further. On hindsight, I realised what a great risk I had taken in physically breaking up the fight, especially since my job schedule cautioned against physical contact with students. Had I not committed a grave mistake? What if one of the students accused me of having hit him in the process? I recalled an incident when a student had falsely accused me of getting his toe squashed by the door when I tried to keep him out of my lesson because of his disruptive behaviour. I wondered who would have been my witness if either boy had falsely accused me. Nevertheless, I handed over the pair to a senior administrator who informed me that one of the boys was a constant headache to the school.

As the school day came to an end, two officials from one of the local banks came to talk to year eleven students about opening a personal bank account. The bank officials were upset by the reception the students accorded them and complained about their nasty experience. It was very difficult to appreciate why students could not save face for visitors, at least. They could be cheeky with their teachers, I thought, but behave better with visitors. No doubt, it was a confirmation of the magnitude of the indiscipline of the majority of students in the school as intimated by the Physics teacher. With such behaviour, I realised what a difficult task it was for teachers to meet their task of teaching without having to commit their greatest energies to class control.

The attitude that teachers have towards students is of fundamental importance if educational objectives are to be achieved. My teaching experience in Uganda, while at Kibubura Girls SSS (a Third World secondary school by Ugandan standards), dispelled the theory that only schools that admit students from socially well to do backgrounds are able to perform very well academically. Kibubura Girls SSS is a rural school whose students were admitted with very low academic scores compared to those of other schools like Ntare. Interestingly, the positive attitude of Kibubura Girls SSS staff who were able to inspire and motivate students in the early 1990s led to the school producing results that were in the realm of the Ugandan First World category schools.

According to *The New Vision* newspaper of 19th May, 1992, the then Minister of Education Mr. Amanya Mushega cited Kibubura Girls SSS among the most improved schools in Uganda, saying, 'School heads should recognise the effort of students from poor rural schools, who in spite of lack of facilities, compete effectively with those from established schools.' The personal article of Alice Nayebare, an old girl of Kibubura Girls SSS that appears at the back of this book is testimony of teachers' significant impact on the students' self-confidence, motivation and inspiration to excel in academics.

The Kibubura Girls SSS success story was attributed to the positive attitude teachers had towards students who would otherwise have been condemned to be Third World material. The students were inspired to have confidence in themselves and to believe that it did not matter which school they went to since the teachers who were handling them had gone to the same teacher training colleges as those in the 'First World schools.'

Indeed, it was not only academic success stories that were registered by Kibubura Girls SSS but co-curricular successes. In 1993, Kibubura Girls SSS participated in the HIV/AIDS district drama competition and to the surprise of many, the students emerged one of the best schools due to their artistic skills and very good spoken English. In fact, there was contention of the results when Mary Hill High School was announced the best school, Kibubura Girls SSS second and Ntare school the third. It was widely believed by many in the audience and other schools of low profile at the time that there was bias towards Mary Hill High School ('a First World school') at the expense of Kibubura Girls SSS ('a Third World school').

The Kibubura Girls SSS success story weakens the argument often advanced in England that students from socially deprived areas, especially the inner cities, are predestined to poor performance. The major problem seems to be in the attitude that teachers have towards the students, as in the case of the Maths and Physics teachers earlier mentioned who have pre-determined perceptions of students' abilities and affirm these in the way they relate to them. The perception of English state secondary school teachers about a student's academic potential based on their social background seems to be part of the English social mentality of the class system.

From my educational experience, I strongly believe that a student from a state secondary school and one from Eton College can compete academically if the teachers from the former school display the right attitude and the students changed their attitude to their studies. There are many state-of-the art state secondary schools that are built with millions of tax-payers' money and which have qualified teachers, who dare motivate the students to do better. I believe the indiscipline of students in English state secondary schools is a symptom and not a cause of poor performance.

It is my contention that if students are self confident, have a high self-esteem and read a positive attitude from their teachers, the fighting, misbehaviour and disrespect of public service officials will hardly arise since their energies will be directed to fulfilment of their educational aspirations, especially through career and guidance services.

CHAPTER SEVEN

COMMANDER OF THE ROYAL GUARD

One of the most potent tools of bringing order into an English classroom, as I was to discover with time, is a loud threatening voice! I never ceased to wonder whether training of teachers provided for this very essential survival skill or if it was developed on the job. I came across many teachers who had to raise their voices and put their feet down to squarely address students' unruly behaviour. In short, a gentlemanly and ladylike attitude does not work.

The loudest noise was made by one of the veteran teachers in one of the schools that I visited. If it had been measured on the Richter scale, it would have qualified for the Guinness Book of World Records. On the morning before the beginning of a school day, as students waited in the corridors for teachers to open their classes, and take roll call, one naughty year eight boy decided to cause a stir by pushing his mates around. Many of them did not take lightly what the boy considered having a laugh, and started arguing with him.

As the tiny little boy continued to terrorise everybody, one tall and well-built teacher arrived, certainly with no expectation of starting his day in style. He was approached by the offended students, who reported the misconduct of their classmate. When he called the boy to briefly talk to him and provide some 'fatherly' advice, the boy refused to come over. As the teacher's patience ran out, he kept on raising his voice until pitch level. Out of frustration at being disobeyed by a young schoolboy, the teacher shouted at the boy saying, 'Who do you think you are?' The almost six foot-tall teacher and the little boy before him provided a spectacle more akin to the Goliath and David story in the Bible.

The noise that was made by the teacher, I thought, could only be matched by the commander of the Royal Guard at Buckingham palace. He erupted into a deafening outburst and the corridor, packed with whistling and jostling students plus teachers, went silent. The sound was like the roar of a lion out of the jungle of Africa. When I reflected on the events of that morning, I realised the teacher's dilemma. He noticed that the little year seven student did not have an ounce of respect for him as a teacher, despite his age, height and muscular build. He must have contemplated his incapacity to administer any effective punishment to the boy. Smacking was certainly not an option and if he had touched the boy at all, the story would have been different for him.

What a patient and cool man he was. I wondered how many people in his position would have resisted the temptation of smacking the little boy. He did not deserve to be in the Guinness Book of World records for shouting loudest but for exercising maximum restraint, patience and self-control. I am not sure whether he followed up the case, but he may have thought twice about it since he might have been taken to task to justify his threatening behaviour instead. The boy must also have counted himself lucky because he could easily have been mauled to pieces that day.

A similar incident happened while I was walking along the corridor of another school, and I heard an outburst from a teacher, who was frustrated with his class. He shouted out at the boys in such a high voice that the noise was easily carried into the corridor. He exclaimed, 'Shush, why do you want to spoil my weekend?' It was Friday afternoon and the teacher's mood for a great weekend was being marred by the students' indiscipline. I never got to know what the problem was but the noise he made said it all. Students anxiously look forward to Fridays with some hope of a break from school, and they in turn cause the teachers anxiety by their restless behaviour.

Many times teachers in different schools would try to organise study sessions tailored to address the Friday fever. Educative video tapes and computer related activities were common. Many times the students whom I would have to teach on Fridays would give me more problems than on any other day. It was, therefore, easy to appreciate the frustration of the 'weekend teacher' but his shout, although not anywhere near the 'Goliath teacher', was in a class of its own.

In another school, my attendance of class in a support role to one of the full-time teachers enabled me to appreciate why many teachers shout at students. The English Language teacher, whose lesson I attended, was a perfect gentleman who did not yell at students at any cost. He was handling a year eleven class and was reading out some very good poems and leading students in a discussion that involved making a literal criticism of each of them. What a good lesson this would have been compared with nice weather had it not been for one unruly girl.

A cheeky girl was to spoil the day with her inconsiderate behaviour that certainly got on the nerves of some of her mates, the full-time teacher, another learning support assistant and I. The girl chatted loudly with a mate and prevented good flow of the reading and discussion of the poems, by the few students who were willing to participate. Almost every two minutes, the teacher would call out the girl's name and pleading with her to behave and respond to the task at hand, to no avail. He remarked at some point, 'Can't you keep quiet for a moment? Today we have some nice weather, why do you want to spoil the day?'

Although at one point I suggested to the teacher to exclude the girl from the class, since her attendance was not being of any benefit except to affect negatively the learning of others, he kept her in class to the very end of the lesson. The teacher must have followed up the matter but I realised how costly it was not to be as threatening to students. Shouting would perhaps have helped. Many times I noticed that students often mistook courtesy, gentlemanly and ladylike manners for weakness. Whenever a teacher tried to be diplomatic in resolving an issue, the students would often rebel.

The indifference of the cheeky girl made me think that many students may have been conditioned to behave well or respond to instructions only after being shouted at or being threatened. But can such induced 'good' behaviour, have a lasting impact on the character of the student? Respect bred out of fear is conditional but respect bred out of mutual regard for each other is everlasting. One thing I was sure of is that 'the gentleman teacher' did not succeed in effective class control as probably a shouting teacher would have, in such circumstances. Yet I thought that his attitude and approach was ideal for promoting respect for the students and that he deserved better from the unruly student. He tried to reason with the cheeky girl in the same way he tried to assist her in gaining reasoning skills in English Literature but she was not interested. Her attitude was what needed redirection, and in that event, shouting at her would not have been the only solution. Nonetheless, I did stop to ponder what a costly business it is, for a teacher, to act in a gentle manner, towards an ungentle student.

The handling of discipline problems in Ugandan schools is certainly very different from that in English state secondary schools. While commander teachers are not totally absent in Uganda, the authority and power that teachers still wield result in many cases being handled through different punishments and on occasions through caning, a prohibited, but stills existent practice in many schools.

Corporal punishment is officially outlawed in Uganda. The use of the cane was banned in 1995 but it continues to be widely used and many believe it instils discipline among students. Many staff still argue for the promotion of a philosophy of reasonable chastisement. According to the *Educamate*, a Kyambogo University Education Journal Vol.2 No.2, a recent study carried out by Kyambogo University lecturers on the effective approaches to discipline in primary schools, found that contrary to the Ministry of Education and Sports ruling on the ban of the cane in schools, pupils, parents, management committees and teachers in that order support the use of the cane. The cane in Uganda is still considered by the majority as a deterrent in the sense that students will avoid doing wrong in order to avoid a painful reward. Perhaps the English commander teacher might not have had to strain his vocal cords if he had had the option of the cane. The only major punishment that seems to be exercised in English schools is confining a student to an Isolation Room for a day or two. In this respect, the student would be separated from the rest and put under surveillance by different appointed teachers who give him or her class work to do.

While I appreciate the psychological impact isolation may cause on the student, who would miss having fun with his or her mates, this kind of punishment does not seem to match the gravity of the problem. The offending student in many Ugandan schools could easily have earned himself a suspension from school of two or three weeks, after which of course any similar offence would lead him out of the school.

The unpopularity of the cane in Uganda has been brought about as a result of its misuse by overzealous teachers who have maimed some students and in some cases have caused death. The general positive contribution of the cane to students' discipline has been attested to by many Ugandan civic and public leaders. Corporal punishment cannot be easily justifiable in the modern educational context and legally, there is a general fear among many teachers and sections of the Ugandan community who believe that without the cane, discipline will be difficult to achieve in schools.

The consideration of other options of punishing students' wrong behaviour, such as cutting grass in the compound, sweeping school buildings, fetching firewood for the school kitchen and so on may also be a thing of the past in view of increased promotion of students' rights and government legislation. With such a trend of events, one can envisage a situation in Uganda where teachers might become as 'toothless' as teachers in English state secondary schools. The results may lead to the emergence of 'commander teachers' with limited options of ensuring discipline among students and the resultant negatively charged academic environment that pertains in English state secondary schools today.

CHAPTER EIGHT

LEARNING DIFFICULTIES OR DISCIPLINE DIFFICULTIES

While there is a lot of professional information on the subject of students with learning difficulties, some of whom are dyslexic, it was difficult for me to appreciate the magnitude of the problem. The bone of contention was that while I was able to cite cases of students who were benefiting from an inclusive education system, there were many other students in the mainstream classes that did not fall in that category, and yet had significant problems with their reading, writing and arithmetic.

During my travels to the different schools, I was often perplexed by the simple exercises that many secondary school students had to do in the different subjects. Many times I wondered why mathematical sums suitable for primary school children, were being given to secondary students, many of whom would complain that they were difficult. Yet several occasions, when I gave year seven mathematical exercises to my seven year old Ugandan daughter, she found them easy.

In one of the schools where I was deployed to teach, a student amused me when I asked her why she could not attempt the numbers I had given her. She said: 'You see, I am a psycho. I am mental and I have a tumour so I can't do Maths.' While I took this for fun, the reality is that the girl did not do my work and she seemed to have real problems in attempting the exercise. What kind of mathematical menu would these students have been treated to in all their six years of primary school, if they were still to be given such simple sums in secondary school? It is not surprising that according to Yahoo! online news, UK, dated 11th January 2007 a discouraging report was made about falling standards of students' performance in GCSE exams:

> Business leaders have expressed shock at new figures showing one in 10 schools were failing to teach 80% of their pupils basic reading, writing and Maths. Four out of five teenagers at more than 300 state schools could not muster C-grades in both Maths and English in last year's GCSE exams according to league tables.

In an E-teach newsletter published on 29th June 2005 (one year earlier than the UK online news report), another lamentation was made by employment agencies about the poor results of secondary school students arguing that 'teenagers with top-grade GCSE passes in Maths and English are having to be tested again when they look for a job because so many lack basic skills.' The newsletter further pointed out that the employers' report coincided with the publication of another report by leading mathematicians saying the subject was in a spiral of decline in state schools.

Mathematics and English aside, whenever it came to lessons like Biology, in many cases, I would find myself giving out some textbooks and exercise books for students to do a particular task. Surprisingly enough, even with some year nine and ten groups (equivalent to Ugandan senior two and three), some students would still claim the questions were difficult, when they only needed to read extracts from the text book and answer the questions. There are not many cases in the wide world, I thought, where students could be treated to such a simple task and still fail to do it or seek assistance. Although I studied

Biology over twenty years ago, I was able to work out the answers by reading the text books during the lesson and yet many of the students, who had just covered the topics with their teachers, could not. I was not convinced that these were all students with learning difficulties and in any case, they looked perfectly alert and astute, save for the fact that many showed no interest in learning.

One of the classes that I handled was particularly dominated by students who were so unruly. I wondered what the dividing line was between students with learning difficulties and students with unruly behaviour. I had thought that many of the students with learning difficulties would be relatively calm and eager to learn. This was not the case, as I was to discover on many occasions.

After handing over a worksheet left behind by a Christian Religious Education teacher for a group of year eight students, some students complained about the difficulty of the task. The task seemed simple to me. It required the students to write out bullet points or a summary on the importance of baptism to Christians. The students disagreed and one of them told me point blank: 'I don't answer questions. I only copy out and anything to do with answering questions is not mine!' Meanwhile, several students paced up and down the classroom, refusing to settle down, despite the intervention of a learning support assistant, who was helping me in the class.

When I consulted with the learning support assistant, she advised me to offer them a much simpler task. I could not imagine anything simpler and wondered how simple such a task would be, what was on the cards. Reluctantly, I accepted the advice of the learning support teacher who said, 'Let them copy out some work.' I was reluctant because I thought it was below their standard, but alas, even that was very difficult for them. A few students tried to copy out some few lines and others refused outright. The few who copied directly from the worksheet complained after some few minutes that it was a lot of work to copy out. Some demanded work involving drawing instead of writing. It was very common with most students in the different schools to expect a teacher to give a task on drawing for the different subjects. It seemed to be an escape route engaging students in some leisurely activity that did not require taxing their minds.

Meanwhile, one of the boys, whom I tried to calm down, and encouraged to write said, 'f*** **. It was quite a chilling message, the first abuse I had suffered in my teaching career. However, since there was a learning assistant in the class, who was a direct overseer of the student's conduct, I thought some action would be taken at this stage. I believed the support assistant would march the offender to the senior administrators, or take him out for counselling. This did not materialise and I soon noticed that the learning support lady teacher was also afraid of the lad. She, like me, anxiously looked forward to surviving another of those bad days.

At no time had I ever thought that some of these students could be high on drugs. In this case, though I was convinced that the boy was not in his right frame of mind to utter such words to a teacher. If he was, I wondered, why did he bother to come to school. I also questioned whether students had 'learning difficulties' or whether many of them had 'discipline difficulties'. Was indiscipline part of the complex definition of 'learning difficulties?' This is an area that I was certainly not sure about, but I noticed that the task of making a difference in the education quality of unwilling participants was not a simple one

Troubled by the abusive boy, I decided to ask one of the learning support teachers to bring in a senior administrator but alas even when the senior manager was invited in the classroom to intervene, he could not get much out of the students in terms of good behaviour. On arriving in the classroom, he found all the 'hardcore' students had their jackets on. When he instructed them to remove them, they refused. Instead, he resorted to instructing one at a time to do so. It is only then that they cowed. However, I wondered, if the students cannot even respect and listen to the senior manager, how could a full-time teacher let alone a supply teacher wield authority in class? These students did not only have problems with meeting the academic demands of their teachers but they had fundamental discipline problems that were reflected in their response to both the teachers and the senior managers.

My Ugandan teaching experience had convinced me that while in a given class students may exhibit different levels of academic potentialities or performance, the English state secondary school experience challenged this theory. The latter reflected a similar pattern of non-responsive students to academic tasks. While I kept wondering why this continued to be so, the answer seemed to lie in the complex interplay between the students' negative attitude to studies and the teachers' resigned attitude to students' academic potential.

While one of the most critiqued aspects of the Ugandan educational system by educationalists is the promotion of teaching methods that encourage rote memory or recall of information, the students are able to respond to given academic tasks in different subjects but, unfortunately, this is not the case with the majority of students in English state secondary schools. Students in Uganda are accustomed to being given tests or exercises whereby they have to answer questions based on work done the previous week or previous year and many of them will often get these right since they are used to revising and 'cramming the facts and theories'. Conversely, students in English state secondary schools were finding it difficult even to read a passage from a Christian Religious Education or Biology textbook.

Surprisingly, some students in English state secondary schools also find it difficult to concentrate on simple tasks like copying work from textbooks into their notebooks. Indeed, while I was able to appreciate the reality of having some students with inherent learning difficulties, requiring special education skills in teaching them, the majority of students I was dealing with were not of that mould. For a First World educational system, I found it quite disturbing that the majority of students could not respond to academic tasks, which would be considered chicken feed to their counterparts in the 'Third World' Ugandan schools.

One of the revealing experiences about the English and Ugandan state secondary schools is when a group of seven Ugandan students from Ntare school visited England with the support of a Rotary club in the south-west of England. The Ugandan students stayed with their English counterparts and attended class with them for about a term. It was quite surprising that the group of seven Ugandan students matched the academic standard of their counterparts and in many cases surpassed it. One Ntare school boy, in terms of marks scored in his class, came top of his class despite attending for one term.

The Ugandan students who visited some schools in England (including one whom I requested to write about his experiences at the back of this book) were astonished at what they considered the 'low academic standards' and aspirations of students in the state secondary schools. Conversely, the Ntare school students were mesmerised (and so was I) when they visited one of the private schools in the north of England. For the first time they met what they referred to as very bright, self-confident students with high academic ambitions and I could not agree more since throughout my teaching experience in English state secondary schools, I had not come across a breed of students matching the ones in the private school we visited.

It is after my visit to the private school that I appreciated the comments that were made by a Conservative member of parliament, Oliver Letwin, who was quoted in the Metro newspaper of October, 10, 2003 as having said that instead of sending his children to his local state school he would rather beg and raise money to send them to a private school! It is in the private secondary schools where you meet students with potential, vision and ambition to make it academically. As for the English state secondary schools, one can dare say it is easier for the camel to go through the eye of a needle than for a student in a state secondary school to make it to university or to another higher institution of learning.

CHAPTER NINE
BATTERED BUT SILENT

Peace does not necessarily mean the absence of war. This dictum came to life when I listened to a story of teachers who had been physically assaulted by students, and yet were not enthusiastic to follow up the matter with courts of law. It is only then, that I realised how lucky it would be for a teacher to survive a left or right hook, from some student at some point in one's career. Sadly enough, though, I came to the conclusion that there are many teachers, who have been physically assaulted at one time by students, but who have chosen to keep quiet.

While having a cup of tea at break time, a colleague supply teacher came over to the staffroom and told us how he had been involved in a nasty incident. He told us that a year ten student (equivalent to Ugandan senior three) whom he tried to block from going out of class pushed him against the door, and forced his way out. He expressed dismay at the behaviour of the boy and wondered what kind of student he was. When he described the boy, the full-time teachers at the school straightaway knew the person he was talking about. As it turned out, problem students were always very well-known in schools. When they referred to a catalogue of offences he had committed previously, it was not difficult to appreciate why pushing a teacher was one of those other things he was used to doing.

What was particularly disturbing from the conversation with two of the full-time teachers at the school was their revelation to us of their own stories of physical assault at the hands of some students. One lady teacher, who was robust in stature, told us how a year ten student had physically assaulted her during a Science lesson. The lady teacher recounted her experience of being roughed up by a mere schoolboy, as she referred to him. She said that all along she had never anticipated such a reaction from any of her students, despite their oftentimes wayward behaviour. The problem arose after the teacher shouted at the boy, who was disrupting her lesson. The next time she came around some of the other students were helping her to her feet. The boy had punched her to the ground.

Surprisingly, the lady did not follow up the matter with courts of law, citing fear of being caught up in a losing battle. She said she was put off by the justice system that she claimed was often unfair to teachers. In any case, she argued she would have no dependable witnesses. I appreciated her dilemma since, after all, she was 'alone' with the students in the classroom. The wise saying that 'birds of the same feather flock together' could not be overruled in a situation where the only witnesses were students of the same class.

More important, she told us that the main reason she shunned going through the rigours of the legal procedures, was that she would end up on a register of offenders. She argued that her record would be tainted, even if she was not found guilty, and as such, it would affect her future job prospects. While her argument was not so clear to me, since she was not involved in hitting back at the student, I was able to appreciate the dilemma of teachers who live in perpetual fear of the students whom they are supposed to teach. She narrated her story as a reassurance to the supply teacher, that in fact, what he had experienced was 'chicken feed' compared to what she had been through. Indeed, my fellow supply teacher must have counted himself lucky after listening to the story. It could have been much worse for him.

Much later on in the same school, I witnessed an incident that perplexed me. As year eleven students came towards the end of their general secondary school calendar year, many of them came to school purposely to disrupt lessons. On one of those days that I went to the school, I passed by a student who was staggering in the school corridors. He was obviously drunk. His white shirt had been signed by his mates, to remind him of them. This seemed to be a common practice among finalists and as well as the passing around of a book for signatures and messages of best wishes.

What was astonishing was the school's decision to keep such intoxicated students in school instead of confronting them and excluding them from the school, at least for the day. When I mentioned the incident to one of the teachers over a lunch break, I was told that the headteacher had advised teachers to retain the students. The lady teacher further informed me that in her year eleven class that afternoon, she had some students who could barely walk because they were high. She said many were just jiggling through the lesson.

It seemed to me that the practice of keeping students at school, even when some were not going to sit for final examinations, was greatly to blame. Why should some students care to learn during the last lessons of the school calendar year when they are not even going to sit for examinations? I was lucky that I did not have to teach a year eleven class during that time and wondered how I would have fared in the circumstances. On a serious note, I considered it risky to teachers to have to contend with intoxicated students, when it was dangerous enough to deal with sober ones. At the same time, it seemed to me that the school administrators downplayed the negative impact of the bad behaviour of year elevens on the younger students. Would they not also follow suit since they would know that it was easy to get away with such indiscipline?

The approach taken in handling students in English state secondary schools where the student is the 'king' or 'queen' and the teacher 'the servant' is proving very costly in terms of fanning indiscipline in schools. This greatly explains why a student can punch a defenceless lady teacher and get away with it. The scenario where the teacher is at the mercy of the students, including suffering physical assault without a way of defending oneself or 'paying back' even through legal means, is a pointer to the unconducive educational environment in a First World educational system.

The Leeds NASUWT (a newsletter publication of teachers) of March, 2003 had a lead article reading 'Child protection; has the balance tipped too far towards the child?' This article lamented the glorification of the rights of the child at the expense of those of the teachers as evidenced in several cases that were won in favour of students. The article in part reads:

> The result of the tipping of the balance is that more and more teachers are having to be ultra-cautious, as this is the best means of defence. Thus we advise male members never to be in a one-to-one situation with a female pupil, nor to lean over to help them with their work. Similarly we advise all members to take particular care when stopping pupils rushing down the corridors.

Whilst precautionary measures are acceptable for safeguarding female students (although no caution is given to female teachers to avoid leaning over girls) against male staff, the physical and mental widening of the gap between a teacher and a student has adverse effects on the teaching and learning process. It is most unfortunate this advice is given by National Teachers Association officials as a remedy to the numerous cases brought against male staff. The advice given can be understood in the context of a sarcastic reaction to a justice system that fails to safeguard teachers from prosecution. The irony is that teachers seem to have suffered more at the hands of students than the other way round.

According to the Leeds NASUWT (teacher's newsletter of April 2003):

> A recent NASUWT survey in the North West showed that over a two week period there were 964 cases of verbal abuse of teachers by students. Similarly, while quoting a survey conducted by a NASUWT official, an undated English newspaper article said pupils attack teachers hundreds of times a day. Almost 1000 incidents of physical and verbal abuse, some by children as young as four were reported during a ten day period in just one region of the country.

Similar to the NASUWT survey, a very recent Reuters news agency report from London as quoted in the Ugandan *New Vision* of February 24, 2004 decries the physical and verbal abuse suffered by teachers in the UK following a survey carried out. In part the report reads:

> Nearly 50% of teachers in the UK are attacked by students. Nearly half of teachers have been physically abused by pupils and more than 90% have been verbally abused. Among those who suffered physical abuse in the latest survey, 53% had been assaulted with a thrown object, 26% with 'weapons' such as furniture or equipment, 2% with a knife and 1% with a gun.

Physically assaulting or verbally abusing a teacher is rare, if not unheard of in many Ugandan state secondary schools. The ugly head of indiscipline in Ugandan secondary schools has been felt in connection with students' strikes and sometimes violent protests against bad food and, in many cases, poor academic performance of the school.

While the indiscipline of students in Uganda cannot be considered better than that of their English counterparts, the question of students reducing teachers to punch bags in a First World educational system smacks of severe anti-social behaviour and social retrogression. The sense of authority of the 'Third World' Ugandan teacher even with the 'barbaric age old discipline symbol of the cane' cuts a better figure for educational advancement than the 'toothless' English state secondary school teacher who is at the mercy of the students and incapable of achieving set educational objectives.

CHAPTER TEN

EDDY MURPHY, LOOKALIKE OR COLOUR BLIND

As a black African, I was to find myself in an interesting position of being among the very few black teachers who teach in state schools. In addition, being a black African (and not a Black British or Black Caribbean) presented me with a unique opportunity of being a player and at the same time an observer of the complex race factor in the English educational, social and political spheres.

One of the most common assumptions that was made by students in White only schools, white and Black British or Black Caribbean plus Asian dominated schools, was that I was from the Caribbean Islands. The misinterpretation of my identity resulted in a wide range of reactions from students, some of which were light-hearted, others nice jokes and others bordering on outright offence. Many times, I downplayed the students' comments, since I knew they lacked fundamental information on the subject of race. But I thought their reaction might not have been taken lightly by someone who was born and bred in England.

The most common question from many students in the different schools that I went to, including ones that had Blacks, was where I came from. It seemed to be a question of ultimate importance to them, while I thought it was not that important. Before I could even say hello to them or introduce myself, the question would always fly out. What is your name? Where do you come from? Are you from Jamaica? As a teacher, I always loved to take them on a journey of discovery instead of giving them the answer. My reaction often was, 'Where do you think I come from?'

Many guesses would often be made about where I come from, but most prominently Jamaica. At such a point, I would tell them that I was from Africa. Mentioning my country of origin was not helpful since many students actually visualised Africa as one big country. I did not blame them. A good number of them had problems with the Geography of their own country. I remember a case where a year eight student was asked to write down the countries that make up Britain and she wrote Island (meaning Ireland), Blackpool and London!

What was particularly noticeable was that the mention of Jamaica would be quickly followed up with the subject of smoking '*Ganja*' a term that I was to become familiar with through my school visits. The first time students brought up the subject, I remember, they asked me, 'Do you smoke?' I said, 'No'. One asked, 'Are you sure, you don't smoke?' Another commented that even if I did, I would not admit it. At this point one student said, 'Do you smoke *ganja?*' I said, 'what is *ganja?*' Another student asked, '*weed*' and I asked: 'What is *weed?*' Another said, '*pot*' and I said, 'What is *pot?*' and another said, '*grass.*' When I asked, 'what is *grass*' another student said, '*hash*'. The list was endless

45

until I told them that what they had described was not completely foreign to me since in my country the term opium was in usage but I told them that it was not a common pastime, and that, in fact, it was not in vogue nor was it used by many people in society.

The issue of *ganja*, which never used to go away, even among Black Caribbean students, provided me with an opportunity to speak to students about drugs. Many students kept joking about the subject and it seemed to me that although some of them could be users, the majority loved to fantasise about them, while others wanted to tease me since they seemed to associate my colour to drug abuse. On one occasion, one student tried to make fun in class by rolling a paper into a conical-shaped object and put some chalk in it for blowing.

When I went over to him and asked what he was doing, he jokingly said, he was making a spliff. When I recognised that it was representation of smoking drugs, I asked why of all games, he wanted to dramatise smoking. Jokingly, without showing a care in the world, he said, 'It is good to show how one can get high'. Since at this point I was familiar with the language of drugs, I sarcastically replied, 'After getting high, what happens next, wouldn't you get low?' Other members of the class laughed off the incident and I asked him to squash his artefact.

I was later to discover that several students loved to draw pictures of a leafy plant at the back of their books or wherever they chanced to put pen to paper. This seemed to be a common representation of the drug world. In all this I thought that the drug talk and its images were representative of rebellion against the establishment and not so much an indicator of drug abuse. Whenever I had an opportunity, I would reflect on the dangers of drug abuse, mainly as a result of the kind of questions and issues they always raised when talking to me.

On one occasion when a student asked my opinion about smoking, I told him that I did not smoke on health and religious grounds. He said, 'You man you a preacher.' At this point I realised how difficult it was for an English teacher to critique any misuse of substances like drugs or alcohol. Although I was just talking about my own experience, the student had already seen me as a 'dangerous person', a preacher, and not a teacher whose business was to teach and not to provide guidance or counsel.

The issue of race took an interesting turn when, in about four different schools, some students remarked that I looked like Eddy Murphy, the popular American film star. Since the remark was made by white students and not black students, I thought that it was possible that it was a case of being 'colour blind'. The one distinguishing characteristic that I shared with Eddy Murphy was the moustache. I had doubts about any other similarity. It was not bad after all, to be a look alike of a famous star actor, but was that an important issue? However, I recalled an incident in which a Black African university student who was known to me astonished me with a grand proposal.

One day the university student came to me and inquired if I had a travel coach card, at which I informed him that I had one. He proposed that I lend it to him so that he could use it to travel to London over the weekend. When I asked him how he would travel using my coach card when it had my photograph in it, he replied: 'When I go to make the payment at the coach offices, those white people will not easily tell the difference.' He continued, 'White people cannot easily tell the difference between you and me.' I was astonished for a moment, not only because of the immoral nature of the act, but because of the striking differences I thought there were, between him and I. He is robust and very dark skinned, while I am relatively slender and light skinned. I did not give him my card, but later I was to learn from another friend that he duped him and used his card. To this day my friend has never received his coach card back.

Notwithstanding the ploy designed by my African 'brother', I came to think that possibly many white people do not easily tell the difference between black people. It reminded me of the comments that I heard from some black people that they often find it difficult to tell the difference between white people and people of Chinese origin. But I thought, maybe this applies in cases where people are of the same sex, similar height and physical features, otherwise there are stark differences between human beings, irrespective of colour, I presume, and with a critical eye one can easily tell the differences.

Despite the issue of mistaking people's identity in the name of colour and the similarities the British White students saw between me and Eddy Murphy, I noticed that there were underlying reasons why students took keen interest in knowing my ethnic origin or religion in the case of Asians. Race issues and racism are realities for the entire English community. So is the question of what religion one subscribes to, especially in the case of immigrant communities that are notoriously religiously sensitive.

The racial stereotyped responses to me, a black African teacher, spoke volumes about the challenges faced by black teachers in English state secondary schools. Apparently, a black teacher is a rare species in English state secondary schools and this is a great challenge to the English educational system since, as in the case of Leeds, a multi-cultural city, there are a handful of black teachers in a sea of black students across the state secondary schools. Without black teachers who might serve as role models regarding academic excellence, the black students seem to have had social psychological roadblocks in being taught by predominantly white teachers.

The plight of immigrant communities in Europe is reported on in the Newsweek magazine of June 12, 2006 that laments the state of education in secondary schools in a lead article titled, 'Europe's failing schools: the continent's educational systems are crumbling'; In part the article reads:

> Less well-known is the fact that many European countries, for all their talk of social equality, foreclose opportunities for education and social advancement.

It is important that the special problem of race is delved into as part of the solution of addressing the indiscipline of English state secondary school students and building their confidence. While the issue of the black teachers is a big one, there is also a need to address that of the Asian community since it is also not common to come across Asian teachers yet the Asian student population is big. Nevertheless, there is a need to address the plight of what are normally referred to as students from inner cities or socially deprived areas. My own experience showed

48

me that, Black or White, students from socially deprived areas suffer a similar fate since they are considered academically weak and these students affirm this by resorting to indiscipline and ruining any chance of developing their academic potential.

While race is not an issue in Ugandan state secondary schools, owing to the fact that student and teacher populations are almost exclusively black Africans, the greatest problem is of tribal and religious identity. While Ugandans show high regard and respect for foreigners of whatever colour or religious creed, they have been generally known to be discriminative to each other on the basis of tribal and religious background. Interestingly, religious discrimination is more pronounced than tribal discrimination, an issue that I explored at length in my doctoral studies.

The fact that the majority of schools in Uganda are religiously founded has led to a silent competition between religious denominations, especially between the Roman Catholics and members of Church of Uganda who struggle to ensure that students are exposed to their respective religious values and ethos and can subsequently vouch for their social, political and economic interests upon graduation. The majority of teachers in most of the religiously founded schools belong to the religious denomination of the foundation body and this is the point where favours based on religion easily creep in.

Despite the trend to recruit teachers who belong to one's foundation body, the academically result-oriented school administrators have often ignored the religious factor and recruited teachers who are known to produce results instead of those who necessarily belong to the foundation body. Similarly the student population is often oblivious of the religious identity of the teacher provided he or she can teach effectively and this is where there is a difference with the English students who are often more pre-occupied with the colour or race of the teacher.

CHAPTER ELEVEN

EXPENSIVE TASTES, LOW ACADEMIC AMBITION

One of the greatest ironies that I discovered with a good number of students that I came across was their philosophy about material things. Through informal conversations that I had with them and observation of the artwork they loved to depict on their workbook covers, I noticed that they had very expensive tastes. However, whenever I contemplated the little effort that many of them put in their work presented in class, I wondered how they would fulfil their life dreams or fantasies. Education is certainly not the only avenue for 'making it big in life' but what enterprise does not call for hardwork, commitment and discipline?

One of the most common remarks that students, in almost all the schools that I went to loved to make about me, was about the wrist watch that I wore. It was a diamond encrusted golden watch, a Rado by make. Countless comments were made in the different schools, but the most common was always 'I love your watch', which of course was a compliment that went down well with me. But this comment was always followed by others, such as, 'How much did it cost you?', 'Is it a Rolex (it seemed they identified expensive watches with Rolex only)?' 'Did you buy it for yourself?' and many others.

What I was able to read into the students' comments was that many of them wondered how a mere teacher could wear an expensive watch. I thought this was an opportunity to explain about working for a good pay in order to afford the good things in life. I hoped many would have appreciated my explanation, which I supplemented with reference to many of their teachers who drove quite expensive vehicles. Some of them seemed to doubt my explanation and perhaps to think that such expensive items were for pop stars or members of other professions. Interestingly, many of them on several occasions would advise me not to wear my watch in public since it could be nicked. They were, of course, more security-conscious than I was and I took their advice seriously.

Another incident that fascinated me about the expensive tastes of students is when I was on a bus to one of the schools and I received a call from a friend, which I responded to. When I picked my mobile phone from my travel bag to respond to the call, there was some muffled laughing on the bus by some of the students of the school where I was going to teach that morning. As I started the school day and moved from one class to another, I came to a class that had some of the students who had been on the bus that morning when I responded to the telephone call.

At one point during the lesson, a student asked me, 'Teacher, what kind of phone do you have?' I said, 'Siemens c25'. I asked, 'Why do you ask?' She said that she had been having an argument with her mate about mobile phones, upon which I told her that they could ask my opinion at the end of the lesson. When the lesson ended they both came over and asked if they could have a look at my phone and I innocently picked it out and showed it to them. They burst into laughter and one of them said 'Isn't it so heavy for you? It is as big as a brick.' I did not take offence but went on to explain my personal preferences and how these determine what I do with my money. I thought it was a good lesson for them but I realised they expected me to have the most expensive phone around, maybe one that could fit in the palm of my hand.

On another occasion, while teaching in one of the schools in the city centre, the class that I was assigned for the afternoon was to attend a careers talk, to help them prepare to make subject choices. The visiting local resource person from an employment agency presented to students a list of professions that included lawyer, receptionist, teacher, hairdresser and students sat in groups of five to reflect on each of the professions and the pay packages attached to each job.

The five students that I sat with started reflecting on what they would do if they were to get their dream jobs. Almost every one fantasised about being a lawyer simply because the pay package was shown as being 40,000 pounds a year. One boy remarked, 'Ah 40 grand that is cool man! I could buy a top of the range sports car.' Each one shared with the group similar sentiments about their life dreams but alas, when it came to explaining the booklet that contained subject choices that they could make (in my estimation to fulfil 'their life dreams'), none of them was that enthusiastic. One student remarked, 'I don't need to make subject choices, what for?' In the boy's world, there was no correlation between his expensive tastes and the kind of education he was to pursue.

What was fascinating to me, was the low starting salary scale of teachers which the resource person indicated as 17, 000 pounds per annum. Isn't the low salary for teachers a turn-off for students? Doesn't it send a message to students that the teaching profession and the education system they represent is that low? I thought this did not 'inspire' students to bestow respect on teachers and was not commensurate with the occupational hazards of the job. I was not surprised when none of the five students was excited by the thought of becoming a teacher. At the end of the day, I thought that teachers deserve much better than the salary they get in comparison to other professions. They do a job which everybody would love to avoid, but which everybody would like to benefit from.

The career talk and the students' disinterest in making educational choices led me to think that the students' attitude to their studies needs refocusing, if they are to benefit from the educational system. Not everybody can make it big in the music and sports industry where millions are made in the blink of an eye by some and not everybody. Big money can be made through other means, but it calls for a positive attitude to work, something that develops in school. This kind of positive attitude was sadly lacking in the students that I sat with on the career and student choice day. What I saw, instead, was their expensive tastes, a good thing but only if it is accompanied by determination to make a difference in one's life. The absence of this determination and positive attitude was the cause of unruly behaviour and lack of respect for teachers.

When I got an opportunity to talk to the whole class after the careers talk, I asked the class what they thought about it and many of them made jokes about the whole event. Of course, often, many students tended to tell teachers negative comments about any educational subject as a joke, to provoke them into fury, or just for a laugh. I went on to give them some dose of advice concerning aspirations and subject choices. One of the students was not bothered, stood up and started walking out of the class.

As I pleaded with him to come back to the class, some of his friends advised me to let him go. I made a sarcastic remark to the rest of the class that 'Any way, he is running away from his own shadow'. When the students asked me to explain what I meant, I told them that running away from responsibility or class work was not wise enough. It was the individual student who loses out and such behaviour might come to haunt him. I said, 'Your shadow is always there with you; can you run away from it?' Later on, I handed in his name to senior school administrators.

Throughout my teaching in Ugandan schools, I always treasured my role of providing guidance and counsel to students whether during school assembly, class time or specially organised sessions. Unlike their English counterparts, Ugandan students have immensely benefited from a host of career and guidance sessions that have fired up students to have high educational aspirations. The desire for expensive tastes is sacrificed on the altar of postponing present day dreams in pursuit of tomorrow's higher long-term goals. It is for this reason that many students from low social backgrounds in Uganda have gone on to excel in academics and to compete with the 'Etonians of Uganda' and beat them on many occasions.

While the majority of Ugandan secondary school students postpone their dreams about expensive cars, phones, houses, and so on, their counterparts in English state secondary schools want to live out their dreams in the present. The dilemma is that while the English secondary school students have wonderful dreams of driving the most expensive cars and living in posh houses, they do not match these or interpret them in light of the educational journey they are on. It is sad to say that I have no doubt in my mind that the majority of the students that I taught in my two year brief stint in England will not achieve their lifetime dreams through education, unless they are lucky to make it big in the market place. On the other hand, I am very optimistic that the majority of Ugandan secondary school students that I taught will achieve (and many have already done so) their lifetime dreams through education.

'Ultimately, what goes around comes around.' The English state secondary school students think that they are getting away with unruly behaviour, but in the end, it is they who will suffer. The future belongs to them, but what kind of future will it be without a good educational foundation in a world that is being driven by knowledge and innovation as opposed to industry and labour? The English teachers in English state secondary schools, on the other hand are beasts of burden and yet the jewels in the crown. But for how long will they withstand the perils of the job? Concerning the Ugandan educational system, what lessons can we learn from our counterparts whom we are fond of aping in all and sundry? Will the Ugandan educational wheel come full circle, following the introduction of free Universal Secondary Education and mindful of the worldwide increased promotion of students' rights? All this is food for thought for people on either side of the Mediterranean.

REFERENCES

E-teach newsletter (June 29, 2005)

Kibubura Girls' SSS Magazine (2006) Nana Publishers, Mbarara.

Leeds Student

Metro Newspaper (October 10, 2003)

Mwesigwa, F.S. (1998) M ed. Dissertation on 'Women, Education and Liberation in Uganda with special reference to Kibubura Girls' SSS', University of Leeds.

Mwesigwa F. (2003) Religious Pluralism and Conflict as Issues in Religious Education in Uganda, Unpublished PhD thesis, University of Leeds.

Newsweek, June 12th 2006, Europe's Failing Schools: The Continent's Educational Systems Are Crumbling, C.T.P Printers, Johannesburg Ltd.

Ntare School Magazine (2000), Nana Publishers, Mbarara.

Rutondoki, E.N., & G.Byamugisha (2006), 'Approaches to discipline in Uganda' *Educamate:* Kyambogo University Faculty of Education Journal, Vol.1 No.1, pp1-14.

The Leeds NASUWT Newsletter (March 2003)

The Leeds NASUWT Newsletter (April 2003)

The Newsweek (June 12, 2006)

The New Vision (May 19, 1992)

The New Vision (February 24, 2004)

The Yorkshire Evening Post (Jan 2001)

LOOKING BACK: THE INDELIBLE MEMORIES OF KIBUBURA GIRLS' SSS

By Alice Nayebare[1]
Published from Kibubura Girls SSS 2005 school magazine with permission of Alice Nayebare

Each of us has cause to think with deep gratitude of those who have lighted the flame within us, especially as we celebrate the 25th Anniversary of Kibubura Girls' SSS. As B.F. Skinner put it: "Education is what survives when what has been learned has been forgotten". I know that some of us can easily forget our origins, our past, live in the shadow of our present and cannot even predict the future. My days in Kibubura Girls' SSS are memorable and worth taking into account when counting my daily blessings and considering my current position in the society I now live and serve. It is undoubtedly apparent that I was founded on a firm, strong and good foundation which was established when I was still of tender age. I joined Kibubura Girls' SSS in 1992 in S.3 and completed S. 4 in 1993 with a first grade. I had originated from a certain school which was the poorest of the poor deep in my home village.

I happened to be a resident of Nairobi House in the first year, and switched to Sweden in the second year. During those days, London, Sweden and Nairobi Houses were topping in cleanliness and, therefore, I am happy to associate with them. While in Kibubura, my life was impacted in many different ways as enumerated below.

Academics

Destined to become a primary school teacher was the highest goal I ever dreamt of. St. George's Teacher Training College was the place I was meant to go immediately after Primary Seven because my father never

---

1 The writer is a lawyer by qualification, Advocate of the High Court of Uganda and at the moment serving as the Programme/Legal officer of the East Africa Law Society based in Arusha, Tanzania.

at our tender age believed in girl child higher education due to early pregnancies of the adolescent girls in secondary schools. Coupled with this, was my poor performance in P.7 where I emerged with Aggregate 30 in four subjects. This greatly aggravated my feeling of being unable and hopeless, lowered my self-esteem and impaired my vision for a brighter future. I thank God that in all that, he had a different plan for my life. My primary school headteacher managed to convince my father to allow me get secondary education up to at least S.4, which suggestion he adopted but strongly warned me that I had to prove my worth of being in school, otherwise he would not pay fees for me.

I joined Kibubura Girls SSS with feelings of inadequacy, worthlessness and I was always humbled by the fact that the highest level of education I would achieve was S.4. Little did I know that my life would turn out to be different and be shaped in a completely different way; neither did I ever imagine that I would live to see my present days. It was in Kibubura Girls SSS where I first learned that girls are as good, brilliant and useful to the society as boys or even better. This featured repeatedly in the Headmistress' and other teachers' daily speeches and addresses at the school assemblies and morning prayers. It boosted my morale and energised my commitment to stage unmatched challenges to the boys in my circles, especially my peers. That was the time I determined to succeed and never bow to our traditional dictates of being inferior as a weaker sex with its associated discriminative treatment. These words in a great measure boosted my self-esteem which has had a long lasting impact in my life (15 years since I left the school). It was with this same confidence that I went to Nyakasura School for my high school and emerged the best student in 1996 from where I joined the Faculty of Law Makerere University. I was always the first for the two years I was in Nyakasura School.

Mathematics was my worst subject but because I had personal care, attention and encouragement to work harder from the teachers, especially the Rev. Sheldon Mwesigwa and our Headmistress Madam Jane Tumusimirwa, I was able to pass the subject with a credit. They believed in me and gently pushed me to face what I found hardest to do. They pointed it out to me that I had the ability to improve and pass the subject. With this unwavering and persistent encouragement, I changed the negative attitude and the deliberate willingness to fail the subject which was so deeply entrenched in me. I will never forget them for this great success I achieved. This motivated me to work harder on the subject and I was able to pass it with a credit which pushed me to a first grade that I had never thought of. With the grade and the results I had got, it became irresistible for my father to yearn for further education for girls. As I write, my father now appreciates and supports the need for higher education for female children and recognises their usefulness to the society.

Teachers

English was the subject I liked most but I needed to be fine tuned in it. I got encouragement from my English Language teacher that if I worked harder, I would certainly get a distinction in the subject. I remember one day he asked us to write a creative composition on the title "The most eventful day". I wrote a story and when we submitted our books for marking, my composition turned out the best and was read to the whole class because it was very good. That greatly boosted my confidence, and I was able to perform even much better thereafter. We were lucky to have teachers who were more interested in bringing out our highest potential in each subject and it encouraged us to work hard.

I remember with great appreciation, that all my teachers were demanding but supportive, caring, and interested in us and our bright future. With great shame and pain, I regret the days and moments I willingly refused to learn and resisted to be advised for my own good. I cannot, of course, forget the times I dodged preps or classes pretending to be sick or hating the most strict teachers for being so hard on me for my own good. If I had another opportunity to be a teenage student, I would appreciate my teachers from a totally different perspective. I am fully convinced that teachers' impact on their students persists, continuing to influence their (students) lives years later - they are indeed indelible memories, indicative of the lifelong influence that a teacher can have.

Spiritual Life

There was a vibrant fellowship in which most of us were founded and we still stand today. I thank God for the then Chaplain (Rev. Mwesigwa) and the team of born-again teachers that taught us the word of God. We used to go for Scripture Union Conferences to different schools and we would also host others. Every Sunday evening, we would fellowship and hold morning prayers every day before classes. We were taught that we should pray as if we had never read and read as if we had never prayed. In so doing we remained trusting God and yet working hard at our success.

It was a good thing for me to know God at a tender age and I am very sure, it never was a mistake or wrong decision to follow him till now. I have found it a big shield against the traps of the wicked one and a greater shelter from all the worldly troubles. Of course the storm and the tempest do come always, but they have found me holding tight on the unshakable Rock of my life. It is God who turned my gloomy life into the bright one that I now lead. I do not know how some other people or even you call Him (God) but I know Him as an ever present and unchanging friend. He has since blessed me with unspeakable blessings and crowned me with his glory and joy and so far the journey has been good and enjoyable. There are so many things I have undeservingly received and achieved not because of my righteousness or hard work but because He is a merciful God. Surely, He takes the poor out of the dust and makes them seat with the princes. I encourage all of you reading this article to accept him as your personal saviour and Lord if you have not yet made that decision.

Health

I happened to be a teenager at a terrible time when the HIV/AIDS pandemic was wreaking havoc and had become an identification tag for Uganda. Young and old alike were dying everyday and the whole country was living in great and untold suffering and terror of the scourge. People closest to our hearts had either died or were hopelessly and terribly sick. The trauma and the stigma were unmatched and evident in people's daily lives. We even thought that a mere handshake was sufficient for one to contract the disease. By then the government was overwhelmed by the numbers of HIV cases, had no simple solutions of containing the spread of the scourge, especially when it came to the young, innocent, unsuspecting and illiterate citizens. It was a life of hopelessness, uncertainty, confusion, apparent fear and despair. Thank God for the then management and administration in Kibubura Girls SSS that relentlessly sensitised us about the disease, encouraged us to talk to our peers about the dangers of the same through drama and music and other means. I thank God today we are alive and we will continue to live and even see better days ahead of us.

Cleanliness

Come every Wednesday after lunch, there was "Keep Kibubura Clean (KKC)". Oh my God! I hated it so much that it would almost make me sick. Oh, how I dreaded that day! But now I fully appreciate the impact of KKC on my life because it taught me to live in a clean and habitable environment and after a while I outgrew the need for supervision to perform such duties and maintain the standards of cleanliness. Our headmistress always taught us about personal hygiene and hard work which made a big difference in our lives.

A word to my sisters

We owe a lot to our parents for providing for us and guiding us in the right way to go. We owe a lot more to teachers because we spend more than 70% of our delicate and vulnerable time being groomed and shaped by them into what we are now or will be in future. If it were not for them, at least life would be different for me. It is for that reason that I think they deserve greater respect, love and attention from their students. When they correct or even become hard on you, always remember that it is for your own good and not out of hate or rejection.

We were all born to succeed, not to fail. Therefore work hard at your success. Whatever you vividly imagine, ardently desire, sincerely believe, and enthusiastically act upon... must inevitably come to pass! I do not believe in Fate, I believe in a Vision for without a vision, people perish.

Eric Hoffer once said: "We are told that talent creates its own opportunities. But it sometimes seems that intense desire creates not only its own opportunities, but its own talents". Therefore, aim at the higher heights, work to achieve and desire a better life than you now live. You should have an ambition, a purpose and a reason to have better days ahead of you. It is only the dead who do not have the above qualities but you are alive and you must choose to achieve.

Conclusion

Teachers should never minimise the role they play in influencing students' lives. Their role is positive, possessing the qualities of a "charismatic adult" who not only touches students' minds but also their spirits - the way they see and feel about themselves for the rest of their lives. Such influence is truly a rare privilege that should be prized and nurtured. Students on the other hand should pay ardent attention to their teachers to succeed.

I would like, in a special way, to remember heartily and deeply appreciate the following teachers for the work well done in my life:

Madam Jane Tumusimirwa – the then Headmistress

Rev. Sheldon Mwesigwa – the then D/Headmaster, Chaplain and my English Teacher.

Mr. Kyakahire Denis – Biology teacher

Mrs Petua Bamanya – History teacher

Mr. Charles Katalihwa – Mathematics Teacher

Mr. Agrippa (our then) gate keeper who did his job with commitment and zeal.

The lioness roars.

Nayebara Alice who wrote the testimony of her studying at Kibubura Girls SSS is now a senior legal specialist with the United Nations Development Fund for Women after serving as Legal officer and Acting CEO East African Law Society. She holds a LLB (MAK), LLM in international law and Human rights from University of Groningen, The Netherlands.

MY ENCOUNTER WITH ENGLISH STUDENTS WHILE IN UK

By Gad Wilson[2]
Article written on request by the Rev. Dr. F. S. Mwesigwa

When I got an opportunity to travel to the UK to visit schools, I did not expect to find students with a generally negative attitude towards education. To clarify on Ugandan student's attitude towards education, right from childhood, children are told that the only way one can survive in the future, is by going to school. Another fact is that, parents struggle a lot to raise school fees and in this case, a serious student cannot play about at school. Coupled with this, is the fact that Ugandan students are in a competitive country where state scholarships and other bursaries are inadequate.

While in the UK, I visited and attended a school for about three weeks. The seriousness of students was hardly noticeable. What was surely noticeable was the teachers' stress after every lesson. Students made noise throughout the forty minutes and it seemed that the major efforts of the teachers were directed to noise control other than teaching students.

My student friends were not ambitious as some of them are in Uganda. For instance, none aspired to be doctors, lawyers, engineers as most Ugandan students would. My best friend Mike told me that he wanted to join a Music and Drama group and he only looked serious whenever he was going to study the subject.

Unfortunately, I was unable to fully analyse the reasons for such a trend of events, perhaps because at that time I was young and experiencing UK for the first time.

---

2   The writer of the article was a student of senior two at Ntare school who, among others, in 2002 was selected to visit a school in the South of England on an exchange visit. Currently he has completed a Bachelor of Laws degree at Uganda Christian University, Mukono.